Your Little Grin

A Children's Book with a Message to Moms
About the Challenges of Motherhood

Written by Amy Shipley
Illustrated by Mandea Brown

Illustration Artist: Mandea Brown
Copy Editors: Paige Welborn
              Donna Lackey
Contributions by: Ryan Shipley
              Donna Lackey
              Stacey Harrell

First Edition: November 2013
Printed in the United States of America

Library of Congress Control Number: 2013906615
ISBN: 978-0-9892942-0-1

Dedicated to mothers facing the challenges of new motherhood,
and to my son, whose little grin melts my heart.

The first time
I took you in my arms,
you were just a little baby.

You were all wrapped up
in your blanket,
and I was wrapped up
in you.

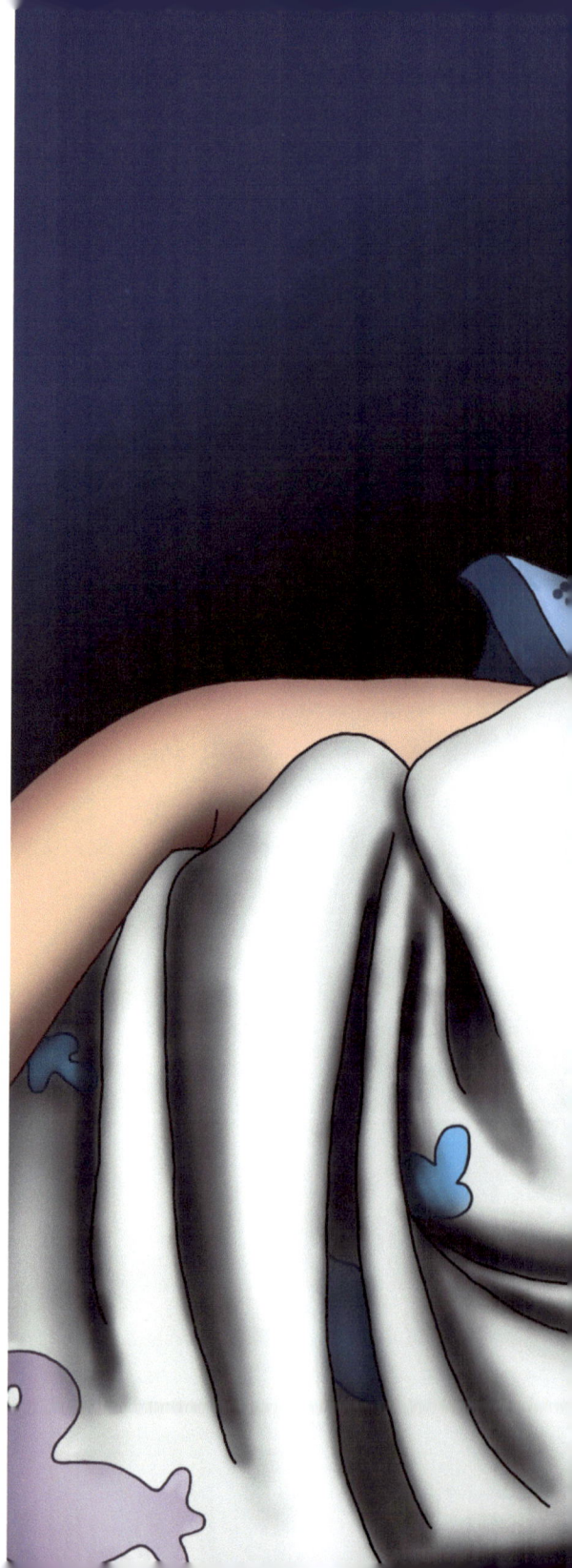

When I looked into your eyes,
you gave me the sweetest grin.

It was as though you were saying,
"I love you,"
and it melted my heart.

When we brought you home,
you didn't sleep much.

You squirmed
         and cried,
                  and I cried too.

I was your mom,
yet I didn't know what to do.

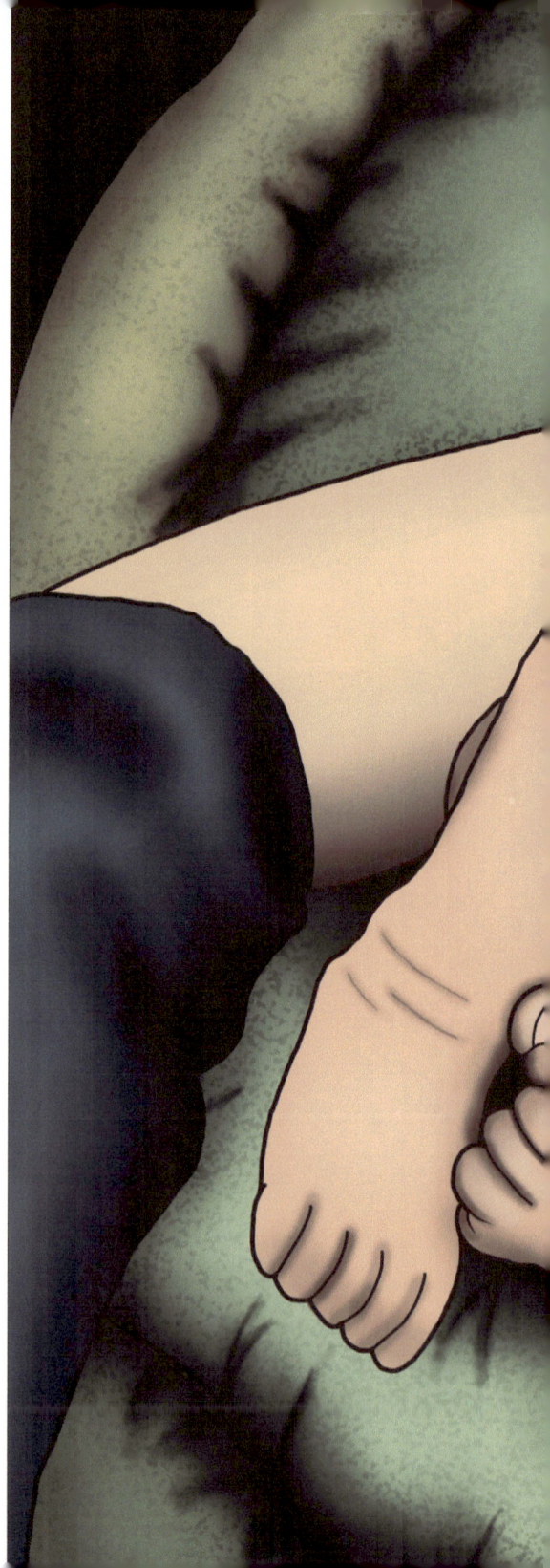

But when I held you close
to feed you,
your satisfied little grin
would melt my heart.

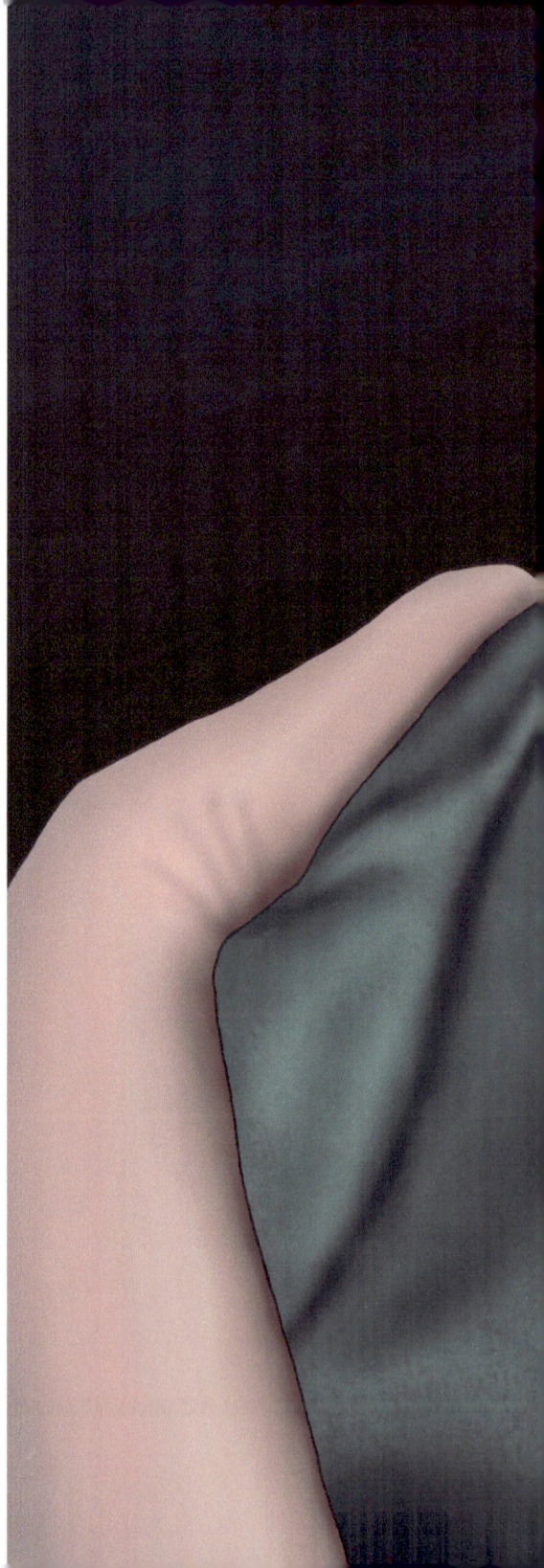

When it was time for a car ride,
you didn't like your seat.

You squirmed
        and cried,
                and I cried too.

There wasn't much that I could do.

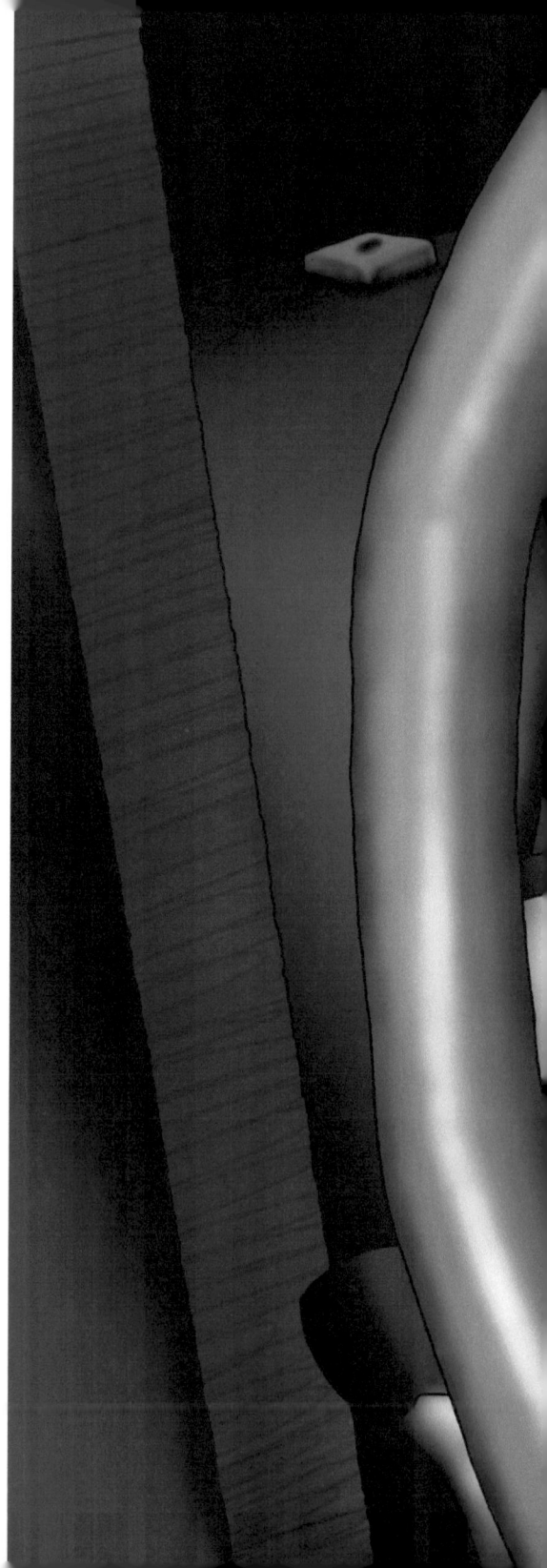

But when we finally arrived
and I lifted you out,
your happy little grin
would melt my heart again.

When it was naptime,
you didn't want to rock.

You squirmed
        and cried,
            and I cried too.

I thought it would be easier
- taking care of you.

But when you finally gave in
and closed your tired eyes,
your sleepy little grin
would melt my heart.

When I had to set you down,
you didn't like to be alone.

You squirmed
              and cried,
                      and I cried too.

I felt so bad for
even briefly leaving you.

But when I came back
and reached out for you,
your welcoming little grin
would melt my heart
all over again.

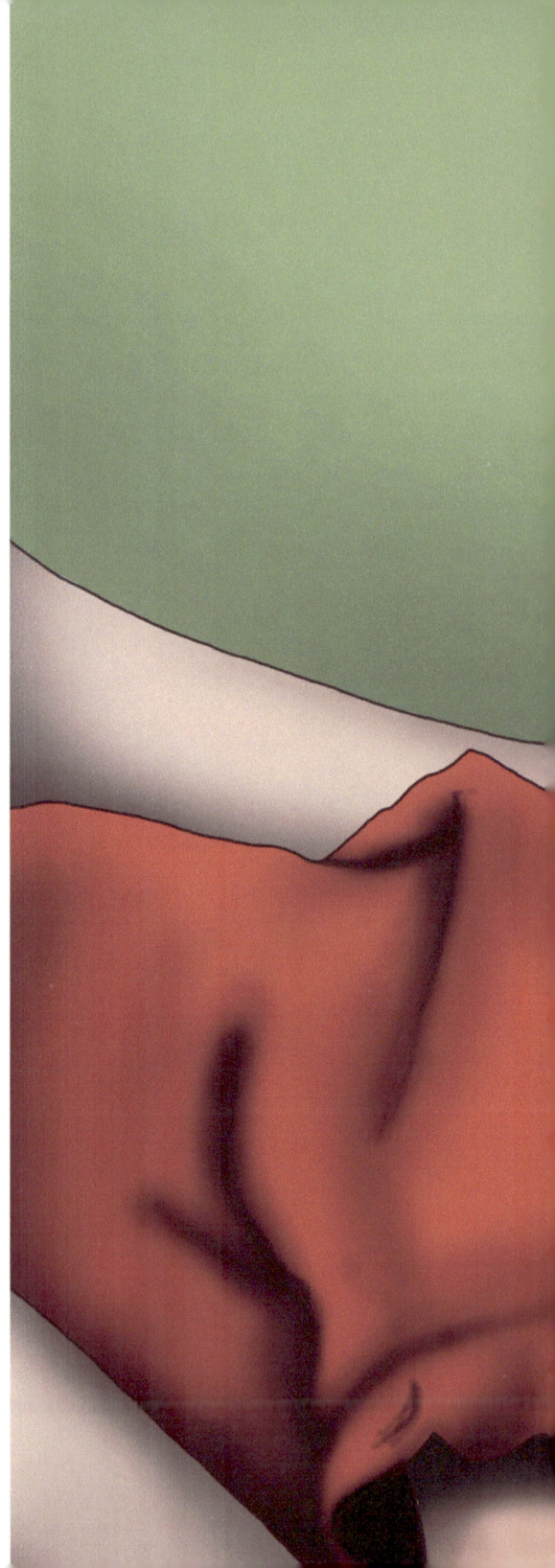

As you've grown older,
the crying has faded.

You giggle
and laugh,
and I laugh too.

When I look into your eyes,
I give you a loving grin.
It's my way of saying
"I love you,"
and you melt my heart
once more.

Now, as I take you in my arms,
you're no longer a little baby.

You're not wrapped up
in your blanket,
but I'm even more wrapped up
in you.

A Note to Moms

Some days are harder than others to feel in love with your baby. During the tougher days, it can be the smallest connection that gets you through. For author Amy, it was her son's little grin. That grin inspired the writing of this book to encourage other moms to find their own connection when coping with the challenges of motherhood. Whether it is finding that special bond between mom and baby, or reaching out to God, family, friends, or a doctor, search out a connection that will help.

These challenges can seem insurmountable when compounded with baby blues or postpartum depression. Many women experience mild, temporary baby blues. Signs may include irritability, moodiness, and sleeplessness. 15% to 20% of women experience postpartum depression.* Signs may include loss of interest or inability to concentrate, changes in sleep patterns and appetite, fatigue, morbid thoughts, and anxiety, as well as a generally not feeling like yourself. Talk to friends, family, or your doctor, and know you're not alone.

The Postpartum Depression Hotline is available 24 hours a day, 7 days a week at 1-800-PPD-MOMS.

*According to Postpartum Support International (htt://www.postpartum.net)

www.ingramcontent.com/pod-product-compliance
Lightning Source LLC
Chambersburg PA
CBHW041222040426
42443CB00002B/60